Richard Barnes

# Mnemosyne

The Orage Press

The Orage Press
16A Heaton Road
MitchamSurrey CR4 2BU
England

ISBN: 978-1-9993680-3-6

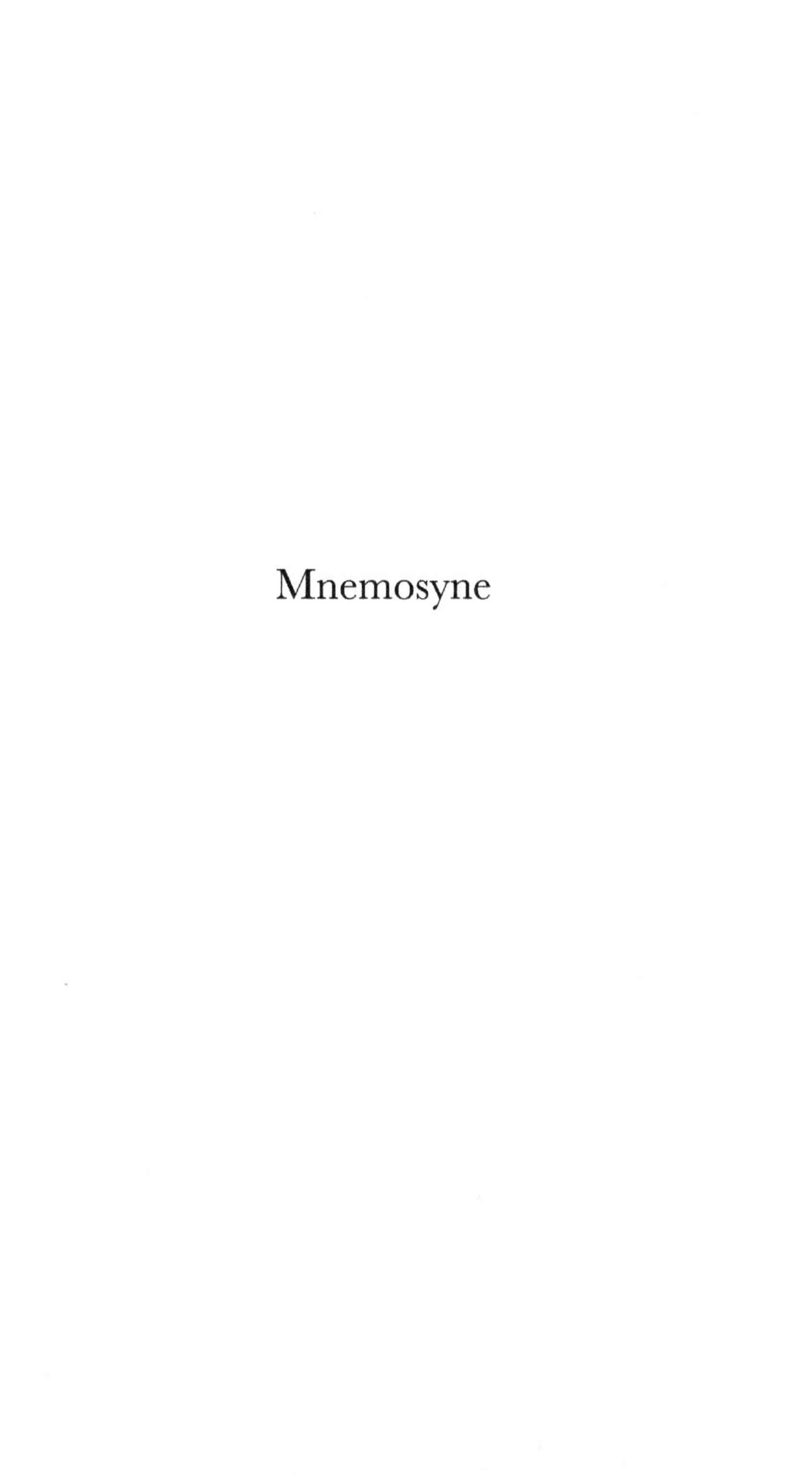

# Mnemosyne

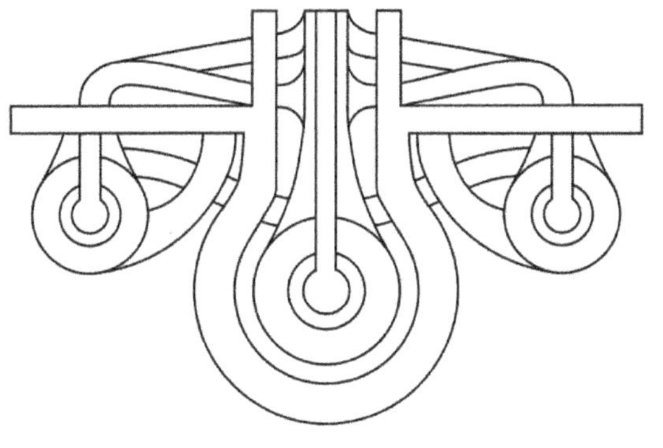

*All of these lines across my face*
*Tell you the story of who I am*
*So many stories of where I've been*
*And how I got to where I am*
*But these stories don't mean anything*
*When you've got no one to tell them to*
*It's true, I was made for you*

Phillip John Hanseroth

# Terpsichore

Like blackened stumps of long-rotten teeth the lignum vitae carcass of piers interminably lost to ebb and flow emerge from the glasslike veneer of the water. The slow list of the boat ramp yaws invitingly away through an uncomfortable acquiescence between land and water.

From heavy antediluvian mists pressing down upon the velveteen surface the spluttered throb of a time worn diesel engine is borne upon the ear. There is an inner comfort to be found in the approach of a ferry, breaking the stillness of sound and sight, day to night, of glass to water.

Time and weather worn, a hulk of former majesty speaks to the senses but not to the eyes. The creative licence darkness affords reflected in the lapping of the water.

# Thalia

Over exposed to light corneal cells crack and blister, the aqueous fragility of its lens-like structure overwhelmed as light floods the retina and damages surrounding tissues. A black spot of macular damage spreads outwards from the centre of vision.

To stare too long into the sun is to invite blindness.

The outward journey, discontinuous, irregular. Stop…start… restart… stop… aimless yet strangely focused, motivated by some hidden cause. Location found, load up swift. Return journey much brisker, disciplined, path memorised, expressed by constance of mechanical alternating gait. Load bearer of precious cargo that offers only partial shade from the rising sun. Leg slips past leg, unceasing in blurred repetition.

A tiny pin prick, now a dark spot, now a shadow across the sun, evolving to full eclipse, day to night in a moment.

Black rust-tinged solleret comes to an abrupt stop. Figure bends double from the waist. Eclipse falls fully over load bearer, who although adjusting course briefly pays no attention.

**"Hmm, what do we have here?**

**"You are a long way from home my friend…**

**"Thought I was the only one here.**

**"What do you have there?**

**"You don't need to worry, you may keep your treasure, I have no need...wondering whether you could give me directions to the nearest... spot of bother on my...no?"**

Path now blocked load-bearer circles frantically in panic of frenzied motion. A slender white flake falls from the jaws, breaking apart when hitting the ground and disappearing against the white background.

**"Oh what have we here?**

**"Don't mind if I..."**

Willowy hand descends to pluck up a shattered portion of the speck, whilst he stares intently at the load bearer.

**"Let me take a proper look at you...**
**"Eukaryota...**
**"Opisthokonta...**
**"Metazoa...**
**"Eumetazoa...**
**"Bilateria...**
**"Protostomia...**
**"Ecdysozoa...**
**"Panarthropoda...**
**"Arthropoda...**
**"Mandibulata...**
**"Pancrustacea...**
**"Hexapoda...**
**"Insecta...**
**"Dicondylia...**
**"Pterygota...**
**"Neoptera...**

**"Holometabola...**
**"Hymenoptera...**
**"Apocrita...**
**"Aculeata...**
**"Formicoidea...**
**"Formicidae...**
**"Formicinae...**
**"Camponotini...**
**"Polyrhachis...**
**"Polyrhachis Simplex..."**

He smiles.

**"Weaver ant!...Really? So far out here?"**

**"Well don't let me keep you fellow."**

Precious cargo retrieved from the ground, firmly clasped once more between mandibles, the ant makes a firm detour around the pointed steel shoe.

Hand raised, fleck placed in mouth.

**"Mmm...sweet...but rain has not fallen here since... so not a gift then?"**

His eyes scan across the empty expanse of salt flat, now blazing white under the risen sun. Then something catches his eye.

**"Oh!..."**

Back straightens, strides some sixty paces, then jack-knife once more.

**"Eukaryota...**
**"Opisthokonta...**
**"Metazoa...**
**"Eumetazoa...**
**"Bilateria...**
**"Protostomia...**
**"Ecdysozoa...**
**"Panarthropoda...**
**"Arthropoda...**
**"Mandibulata...**
**"Pancrustacea...**
**"Hexapoda...**
**"Insecta...**
**"Dicondylia...**
**"Pterygota...**
**"Neoptera...**
**"Paraneoptera...**
**"Hemiptera...**
**"Sternorrhyncha...**
**"Coccoidea...**
**"Pseudococcidae...**
**"Trabutina...**
**"Trabutina Mannipara..."**

Craning down further, ostrich pose, face practically grazing the ground.

**"Ah, good morning madam!"**

Hand moves to doff imaginary hat.

**"Sorry to disturb et al, yet I couldn't help but notice... just passed an acquaintance of yours or so it seems."**

Almost indistinguishable from the bleach-barren surroundings a white filamentous form lumbers along, in appearance some strange hybrid of popcorn and polar bear, though in size merely half that of the load bearer. Trailing this ponderous perambulation a slow extrusion of sticky substance that gently hardens in the sun to form white flakes.

**"Please don't think me too forward but..."**

Tip of lissom finger dipped into the viscid trail and then delicately placed on the tongue. Lines of confusion unfurl across the brow.

**"But nothing has grown here since...well since... before...but if you are here... then... there must be something more..."**

Another finger tip extends and in one movement scoops up a hardened flake and pops it into his mouth.

**"What am I missing here?...Complexities certainly... sweet nectar of the... I must complement you on that my lady! But wait, what is this...hints of...of... tamarisk!"**

Raising his eyes he gazes out across the terrain, but a moment later lets this fall unreturned once more to the ground.

**"but there's more...an older hue...something nobler of intent, subtler... saline soils, yet woody, smoky even...burnt? Burnt ash, soda ash...fizz...baking soda? Salt, soda ash, baking soda...**

He freezes as a new thought dawns.

**"Netjry...natron?...It can't be...not here...though... perhaps not manna from heaven, yet heaven from manna indeed...As above so below...we can taste the universe in every bite..this is all too delicious!"**

A hollow dusty chuckle raises from somewhere within.

**"Thank you madam...thank you indeed!"**

Straightening once more, in a trice he is off towards the horizon, a dervish trail of tiny white cyclones kicked up in his wake.

***

Fore and aft the salt flats spread, barren expanse but for his presence, an uncommon occurrence afloat 'pon this tranquil albino sea. Mirror-matched yet horizon cleaved, consonant twin ocean of deep azure sky crowns the stark white brilliance of this empty plain.

And into this calm, breath. The air appears to breathe. Fuzzy bend of mottled pregnancy, heat shimmer of expectation.

He waits.

Descending coolness, inversion. Nothing seen, then nothing more begets belief that nothing is to be seen. Yet there is a seeming. The empty horizon seems barely able to contain nothing but itself. And in a moment the nothing bends and buckles against itself. A something, a shimmering Rorschach blemish against the sky.

Blink.

Shift of form and shape, one moment this, one moment that.

Double blink.

Three dark blots stacked one atop the other, then gone.

Focus shift.

The same shape inverted, stacked four high.

**"Mistress of the fairies of the salt sea...Fata Morgana?"**

His voice trails off as the image disappears. The vista empty once more. Turning his body he starts to walk towards this coruscate form.

***

Slender branches amid grey-green foliage flex soporifically in the breeze, moving rhythmically under the weight of a dense mass of pink-white blooms.

**"Eukaryota...**
**"Viridiplantae...**
**"Streptophyta...**
**"Streptophytina...**
**"Embryophyta...**
**"Tracheophyta...**
**"Euphyllophyta...**
**"Spermatophyta...**

**“Magnoliopsida…**
**“Mesangiospermae…**
**“Eudicotyledons…**
**“Gunneridae…**
**“Pentapetalae…**
**“Caryophyllales…**
**“Tamaricaceae…**
**“Tamarix…Ahh, the mighty tamarisk!”**

Approach tree, circle three, no, four times, then head tilts to one side with avian-like intent. Focusing on the purplish bark, the searching gaze becomes locked upon a single point. What appeared still now suddenly alive with tiny popcorn spills.

Tap-tap-tap against the trunk.

**“Now where do we think?”**

Knuckles become methodical dowsing rods.

Rap-rap-rap.

**‘Hmm.”**

Rap-rap.

Knock.

Halt of furtive hands.

**‘Ah!…The source…but how to?…”**

Pause.

**"Method of extraction?"**

Solleret kicked off in an instant like an unwashed sock, its tapered point used part peen, part claw to strip the outer layer of bark from the tree. The uncomfortable acquiescence of wood to steel transmutes under deftness of hand and tool as anfractuous fibres begin to part and a way through is found.

Pick-pick…rip…pick.

Bark to cambium, phloem to xylem, sapwood to heartwood.

Thud.

Something hard struck.

Clunk.

Cessation of activity.

**"Well well."**

The corner of something unearthed. With renewed vigour he continues to strip away the tree from around this unnaturally lodged object. Stopping, stooping to gather up some long fallen branches and pile them perfunctorily next to the site of activity, he then returns to the former task and with gentle almost reverential lightness of touch and a tenderness at odds with the harsh surrounding environment reaches into the tree and delicately looses the large casket from its wooden coffer. Tipping its end towards himself, with the assistance of gravity he lays it venerably down upon the gathered lignum vitae carcass of biers.

Interminably lost to ebb and flow, the curved contour of the coffin lays once more revealed to the light. Adorned with hieratic forms, glyphs proud indecipherable strokes of knowledge long lost, of times before and times beyond those yet to come. Opening the lid he reaches in, and from beneath the high gentle curve of feathered Atef reverentially extracts a skull. Blackened stumps of long-rotten teeth illumined by the sun.

**"Hello old friend, I wondered where you'd been."**

Placing this to one side he reaches his arm down towards the torso. Bejewelled material splits and disintegrates falling to dust under his touch. Hand pressing further, deeper, down through fibrous primordial interplay of skin and tendon that cracks and splinters, yielding fracturously to his fingers. Reaching the object of his search he curls his fingers and pulls forth the jet-black spine, thrusting his prize-filled hand skyward.

**"Behold the Djed!"**

He shouts dramatically to no-one.

**"She hasn't found you yet!"**

A dusty chuckle rattles from deep within.

Laden with sweet mists of manna shook loose from the tree, the air hangs heavy yet motionless, a single frame of time sliced from itself that lasts too long. A breath of air trembles the flakes to whirl and whorl, to fall like the whispers of a first snow. Yawing from endless slumber the firmament opens, a single raindrop cuts a direct line down through the mingled whiteness, exploding against his unshod foot.

Time breaks and the deluge begins. Sight is swallowed in the mingled dust of heaven and earth.

From crown of tree two dark forms stir. Obsidian glisten as droplets run rivulet off oil-preened feathers. Wings unfurled and shaken in this most unexpected of showers. Slender branches flex deeply as they take the air and in a moment the two ravens alight upon his shoulders.

**"Hello my beauties, how have you been?"**

The reply softly chattered.

**"It is time...go find him."**

With that they are gone, mere calligraphic streaks against darkening skies.

In one fluid motion he closes the casket lid against the rain and straddles this long dormant steed. Time and weather worn, a hulk of former majesty, the coffin now loosed from earthly grip begins to float once more as the water rises.

The sun is dowsed and all is swept away, the creative licence darkness affords reflected in the lapping of the water.

**"Antediluvian mists indeed..."**

# Clio

*On a lonely plain, far away from the life of to-day, stood once the sumptuous villa of another Emperor, who had brought the sphinx from the banks of the Nile to adorn his garden. Of the palace nothing remains but a heap of stones, but deep in the bowels of the earth still lies the sphinx. Search and you will find her. It will nearly cost you your life to bring it here, but you will do it.*

*(Munthe, The Story of San Michele, 1929)*

## Thursday 7th June 1984

Slept very well, we both did. First time all week. The alarm woke us at 7:30. Difficult to get up. We got the coach at 8:30 for a tour to Pompeii. Felt the guide could have shown us more. In afternoon the coach took us half way up Vesuvius. We walked the rest. Hard climb, but well worth it, fascinating to see the crater and lava flow from 1944. Went to a cameo factory on the way back to the hotel. Didn't get anything. 'A' took some pictures of the hotel from the quay. I read a bit. In evening read, bed about 11. Very tired again. The evenings go very quickly.

Effort to walk on ever-shifting surface. Waded struggle up pumiced switch-backs grey to red…no matter! Half-skipped, half-ran up to crater rim. Pockets soon deep treasuries of assorted chunks of blackened scoria. Fumaroles breathe a steady mist from deep within the cone. Sulphur in the air, as large hands sit us on rocks near spewing vent. Turning to make our descent 'P' who waited at the coach - thinking the climb too much, emerges triumphant through mists after he thought he would have a try.

Wed 6th June 1984

Had a grim night. Didn't sleep at all well. Sore throat and cold. [...] After breakfast we did some shopping. Not nice out. Cloudy, much colder and rained a bit late afternoon. We came back to the hotel. Washed my hair, did some washing, read. The boys played. We had lunch out. In afternoon went to Herculaneum. Covered by mud from Vesuvius. It was very impressive, even furniture left. Got stuck in traffic on way back. In evening read. Bed shattered about 11. Hope I sleep better tonight.

Tuesday 5th June 1984

[...] We hired a car - 'P' drove there, 'A' back. We left about 10:30, drove along the coast road to Positano and Amalfi. Stopped at the Emerald Grotto - boat in a cave. Lovely views on the road. Went through Salerno to Paestum - Greek temples and Roman town quite interesting. Home via motorway much quicker. In evening read. Bed about 12 - tired full of cold. Pleasant day, holiday nearly over.

Grotta dello Smeraldo, wide boat oared by strong men, tokens paid. Sway and yaw, pitch and surge, driven onto the rocks by rolling water, or seeming so, yet threaded deft under and through jagged maw barely open to tide. Now into the dark undark. Subterranean aurora plays soft to dance 'pon cavern roof. Peer over gunwale down to crystal depths, refulgent smagardine lume peers distant back.

Hypnos-led, drawn wide-eyed through waking slumber I roam away around peripteral steps. Lured through imagination by

the rules of some complex game, now alone, enthralled to wander another realm. Jumping up and down from step to step, one level to the next then back. Up and down between the steps and the tall grass I disturb a snake, and fearing flee.

Euthynteria…
Stereobate…
Stylobate…
Crepidoma…

Back up between the nine, hide safe behind entasic spread of fluted skirts.

Anta…
Pronaos...

Relief of familial safety, danger forgot. Run and laugh again.

Cella…

To play once more within the innermost of innermosts.

Adyton…

In Hera's heart.

## Monday 4th June 1984

'A' again had a restless night. We got up at 7:30. 'A' decided to stay at the hotel. We all went to Capri for the day on the hydrofoil. Took 15 mins, left about 9:15. Already crowded when we got there. Got much worse. Went to Anacapri. Saw the Villa of San Michele. Lots of waiting around and time wasting. After lunch saw the

gardens of Augustus and Gracie Fields house (roof anyway). Lovely shops in Capri no time to look. Had a small boat trip round half the island - quite interesting. Hydrofoil back by about 5. Could have been a better trip. 'A' seemed weak but better. Bed about 11 very tired.

Do you remember that day trip to Capri? Did we look around a church?…Or was it a house…or a large villa? Some archeological remains perhaps? I know it was very high up, you could look down across the island, out to sea… Do you recall? Vague notions that in the past people had been flung off the balcony…by the emperor? Oh I don't know…the details are just so difficult to…

I remember only a lion sat atop a parapet. Something about touching the lion and making a wish.

Do you recall?

Time and weather worn, a hulk of former majesty. Tailed mottled pink granite haunches rubbed smooth. Ribs visible, under taught stone skin, nape of nemes between shoulder-blades. Recumbent pose upon the chapel terrace wall. Facing away, out seaward to the horizon. But her face…her face? From whatever angle you approach or try to lean out over parapet at dizzying height, you can never see her face…her gaze. And a sphinx without a face is…well is just a lion, facing eastward, towards the rising sun.

*But this most curious mongrel here,*
*this changeling, a lion and woman in one,-*
*does he come to me, too, from a fairy-tale,*
*or from a remembrance of something real?*

*(Ibsen, Peer Gynt, Act IV, Scene XII)*

Legend has it that if you rest your left hand on the sphinx and make a wish whilst looking out over the sea of Capri, your wish will come true.

Holding tight to metal handrail of steep white steps that spill out over tumble-down cliffs to azures far below, I descend to the next terrace, lines of concentration unfurl across my brow. Mind Charybdic whirl of thought about gravity of decision just made. For moments ago, on very tip of toe, arm raised high above head, my left hand makes grazing contact with the recumbent flanks of her cold granite form...and in doing so I make a wish.

So now the burden of celestial weight sat square upon the shoulders of innocence, and I some tiny Atlas, entrusted with this Herculean task. For wishing is a serious business before we come of age, imaginations dulled with Reason. In a world lived as yet carefree, thus far unshackled to the possible, to the burden of rule, we Knew then that wishes do come true. That such requests to the infinite are answered in kind. And if we through age and reasoned mind have stepped away from the possible, and in the now, not there-between, could know the weight, we would not proffer them so freely, yet best leave it to those who know too well the price, that lie between the now and then, some luricawne or vesseled djinn.

I do not recall the wish I made that day all those years ago.

The wish I made…
Wish I made.

Wish.

No…something's not right.

Speaks to the senses but not to the eyes.

*Do not ask me any questions, I cannot tell you, I dare not tell you. You may ask the huge granite sphinx who lies crouching on the parapet of the chapel in San Michele. But you will ask in vain. The sphinx has kept her own secret for five thousand years. The sphinx will keep mine.*

*(Munthe, The Story of San Michele, 1929)*

Try again.

But careful now, for there is a limit to that which I can recall, no matter how oft I retrace my steps, and beyond that I fear to go lest edges blur from that which was to ne'er before. I must wary tread a careful path, for now I walk a Chinvat bridge. If I should build on shifting sands, then what of the next and the ones to come? Will time like tide wash away and crumble down that which I hold most dear? Or planting seed of conjured vine, to bind the shifting dune, roots curl to cradle my dearly held, whilst up above swift grow to splendid tree, with ripened swell offer too soon the fruits to pluck. First bite, first Fall to knowledge woke, yet this the next away. Too easy now to taste the flesh, to fall to forgotten slumber of memories once sacred held.

I must hold my line, nor stray the path…I must.

So with gentle almost reverential lightness of touch, I reach in to the tree…Clamber-crawl, down through gnarled twist of roots, insidious now, that bind too tight and strangle-crush, buckle-fold memories to collapse upon themselves. With snicker-snack of vorpal blade, I cut steadfast through swath on swath.

Creation, recreation, creation.

Down again and further still, path runs slick from heel to toe, yet slither-slipper down. For here I dwell and choose to walk uncertain amongst the shades. Footfalls on the boundary of another world.

Turning my gaze back to whence I came, slender branches flex deeply as They take the air. My eyes leave my eyes, yet sight I have still, to look down upon myself, to view that which I have done.

Speaks to the senses but not the eyes.

Sat proud, whiteness of walls, blueness of sea. Vivid yet gone.

Recumbent?…Sat proud, arch of back.

Sat proud, I cannot see her face…her face.

I cannot see her…

*Hundreds of huge bats were hanging in black clusters round the walls, others were fluttering in wild flight round my head, blinded by the sudden light of the torch. In the midst of the hall crouched a huge granite sphinx, staring at me with stony, wide-open eyes . . .*

*I started in my sleep. The dream vanished. I opened my eyes, the day was breaking.*

*(Munthe, The Story of San Michele, 1929)*

Small square white mounted pane, Framed slice of time. Chromogenic dyes on acetate sheet. Window to the past. Between thumb and forefinger, arm raised high above head, towards the light. Lambent dapple thrown soft across my face from some tiny stained glass portal. Ephemeral presence of the past in the present.

There was a time when a photograph couldn't lie.

Sat proud, whiteness of walls, blueness of sea. Vivid not gone.

Lion…

Not gone.

Lion…not lion, for this one has a face…and wings

Sat proud. Vivid.

And a lion with a face and wings is…well is just a sphinx. Facing westward, towards the setting sun.

Damascene swing of felling blow. Sharp exhale of breath, carry-sweeps autumnal fall to clear the path.

And there, chemical stain cross sheet of time. My mother, younger than I today. My brother and I… I, six nearly seven years old. Standing against white parapet wall gleaming in the sunshine. Expanse of blue sea stretching behind to rise mirrored at horizon. Mop of blond hair atop striped coat, shorts and red laces. Arm raised to the level of my eye, small hand clasped around foreleg of stone sphinx, sat proud atop parapet wall. No trace of recumbent granite here, she up upon her marbled haunches, wings unfurled, ready for flight. Arch of back echoed in curve of breast, sat proud, waiting. Focal point of family group through gaze of lens, returned inscrutable beneath fullness of hair…Her face…westward framed by risen sun. Sat proud, my lion not lion, my sphinx…Time and weather worn, a hulk of former majesty, my Etruscan splendour…

…Speaks to the senses and to the eyes.

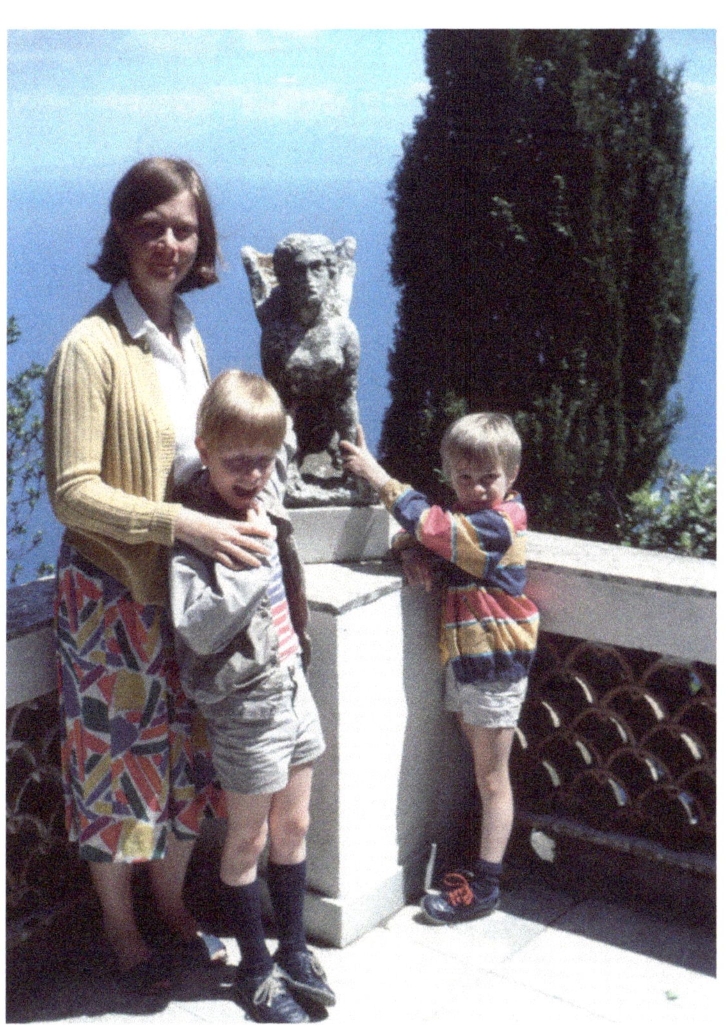

# Erato

Like blackened stumps of long-rotten teeth the
lignum vitae carcass of piers
emerge from the of the
water. The slow list of the boat ramp yaws invitingly

between land and water.

From heavy antediluvian mists pressing
surface the spluttered throb of a time
worn diesel engine is borne There is an
in the approach of a ferry,
breaking the sound and sight,
of glass to water.

Time and weather worn, a hulk of former majesty
to eyes. The creative
licence affords lapping of
the

# Euterpe

*How strange now,--I really fancied there came*
*from the statue a sound. Music, this, of the Past.*
*I heard the stone--accents now rising, now sinking.--*
*I will register it, for the learned to ponder.*

*(Ibsen, Peer Gynt, Act IV, Scene XI)*

Time and weather worn the rope that binds. Frayed now down to the very last.

Up

From the fathomless they hap, breaking the stillness of sound and sight, day to night, of glass to water, towards this hulk of former majesty,

Up up

now the clamber-climb 'pon Jacob's ladder, slither-slide across the deck, to pluck and maul, to rake the flesh, to reap amongst the weary crew. Then on, half-scantling length in blink of eye.

Thrice round the mast they wheel, then thrice they roam, closer yet through every turn. Foul breath too close on nape of neck, feathered spall across the cheek. Then glimmer-glint thru gloom the taloned claw. To tease and tug 'pon remnant of braided twist.

## Fetter-Snap

The sharp retort of final thread that cracks across the lonely prow, that scatter-startles away, with force that cleaves the air and rives the waves to shock the deep with seismic shift,

Marsili.
Palinuro.
Alcione.
Lametini.

Sweeps wide ’neath Tyrrhenian sea.

Eolo.
Enarete.
Sisifo.
Magnaghi.
Vavilov.

So swift along Campanian arc, to roll out across Phlegraean Fields, and sound a knell that echoes through Avernus’ depths. That welter-stirs the long quiescent sleeping throng who lay deep and warm within Erebus’ breast and rouse Erinyes’ bloodshot eye, beneath the fertile dome.

*On the 24th of August, about one in the afternoon, my mother desired him to observe a cloud which appeared of a very unusual size and shape. He had just taken a turn in the sun and, after bathing himself in cold water, and making a light luncheon, gone back to his books: he immediately arose and went out upon a rising ground from whence he might get a better sight of this very uncommon appearance.*

*(Pliny the Younger, Letter to Tacitus)*

My father was ill that day.

My mother, younger than
I today, took us, my brother and I…
I, six nearly seven years old,

by ferry - hydrofoil, to the Isle of Capri.

First time away from the country. First time on a plane. Went up to meet the captain in the cockpit. First time amongst musical language not of our own.

Up and down…

…between the steps and the tall grass I disturb a snake.

Highest pinnacle of the world, highest I had
ever been or known…

…Smagardine lume peers distant
back.

We will not jump unless
pushed.

At the corner of
the parapet…

…she sits.

My mother's hands on my ribs, lifting me beneath the arms, gentle yet fully within her grasp. Hoisted up to give a better view out over the expanse, so I can peer down over the edge of the balustrade. And as the world falls away, so too does the pit of my stomach as I look down over chasmic drop from parapet, down over falling landscape that tumbles free of vegetation to grey white cliff, out and down to bright azure sea some thousand feet below. And as I gaze, something new, a need, an urge that wells from deep within.

L'appel du vide.

Rising on breath of wind a distant voice that swells sonorous upon the tide. And now the next abrades the first and then the third, laid jagger-clash to rest unstable 'pon the ear. Voice joins voice on voice in this tritoned cacophony.

Augmented fourth, diminished fifth, within the evanescence of some tinnital dream. Barrage of sound, infernal din, bred of Nyx this Erisian tone. The hook that lures through tensions built, this rolling call from Sirenum scopuli. Too much to bear, this shuddered dissonance, that draws the ear, turns tauter-twist the mind hair's breadth from Maniaes' grasp.

At the corner of the parapet she sits, immobiled as from a gorgon's stare. Yet now borne soft from those cold hard lips that

lay beneath the stringent gaze, the faintest tone begins to stir, billow-swell to marbled peal, rings crisp and clear to cut through keening call, out across the bay of Naples. To quell-resolve the rising hornets nest of sound that gnashes 'gainst the tide, to final perfect cadence, gifted tintinnabuli from Concordia's fair hand.

L'appel du vide.
The call…

From that day on I've heard it hence, each time I climb to lofty heights, tread spiral steps of soaring tower, or walk a cliff-rimmed path. I feel it now, the lure. She sings and calls me back across this chasm of time, draws me through remembered pasts, that maunder from truth through reinvented whim of where I've been and what I've done. Back, back to that time and place beside the parapet.

And if I now should take my mother's place, should step into her shoes, place my hands as her hands upon my ribs to lift my younger self beneath the arms and lean me out so I can gaze down to chasing depths, to feel this vertigo of possibility open wide beneath me and glimpse the possible gaze back once more.

What then?

If I should once more hear cadent call of my Etruscan splendour and sisters out across Tyrrhenian sprawl?

Then…?

Then I…

I, like some modern day Tiberius, should cast my young self out, Icarian weight flung wide from parapet, out to fall upon the rising wind.

# Melpomene

Bolts drawn back, doors flung wide to startle-scatter meandering bob of pigeons. Upon dying strains of Missa solemnis heavy hung on stagnant air, the procession surges out from dark incense'd depths through green central doors to bright light of day 'neath glaring white baroque facade, spilling forth to red-tiled piazzetta. A murmured hush falls with first glimpsed lurch-sway of shouldered burden not burden, rather honour bestowed, of careful shuffled-step out across threshold worn smooth by the faithful. Muzzle-burst laudations spill out from jubilant mass as He is borne aloft to be carried high above the crowd.

For on this thirteenth day of July, this Festa Di Sant'Antonio, the carved figure adorned but once a year in mantled finery, with deep brocade bejewelled with gilded hue that cascades around exalted form, makes a slow listing perambulation of parish boundaries, bearing forth His divine influence on the community, as He claims them for His own.

Via Giuseppe Orlandi.
Viale de Tommaso.
Via Caprile.
Via Pagliaro.

On and on through twister-twine of throng-laden narrow cobbled lanes, festooned in decored wonder. The seven ages of woman and man, crammed hodgepodge in every door-well and jamb, bear guantiera laden with sweet profusion of blooms that overspill finely decorated altars made special for today. Bands strike up to colour the air with sound that percolates the constant toll of bell and firecrackers' peppered rat-a-tat. From

gaping windows high above, hands fling petals of broom, that rain down upon the tonsured pate, fragrancing the air with delicate ginestra'd scent.

Amidst this mingle-fall, this blaze of colour, one single mote winds and wends a slower yet heavier path, and from feather-soft of darkened form, the fetor of sulphur, astringent peeve that lingers 'pon the nose. Then another and yet one more as the air begins to haze, to yellow and darken. Sweet ecstasy of revel succumbs to anguished jeremiad, as ash and pumice begin to rain down. Time breaks and the deluge begins. Sight is swallowed in the mingled dust of earth and heaven. The sun is dowsed and all is swept away.

And through the darkness, a wing, swept long and low, feathers glisten ebon around.

*You might hear the shrieks of women, the screams of children, and the shouts of men; some calling for their children, others for their parents, others for their husbands, and seeking to recognise each other by the voices that replied; one lamenting his own fate, another that of his family; some wishing to die, from the very fear of dying; some lifting their hands to the gods; but the greater part convinced that there were now no gods at all, and that the final endless night of which we have heard had come upon the world.*

*(Pliny the Younger, Letter to Tacitus)*

# Calliope

*'That time-worn Doric order—a lovely thing—I have the cheek to adopt. You can't copy it. To be right you have to take it and design it…It means hard labour, hard thinking over every line in all three dimensions and in every joint; and no stone can be allowed to slide. If you tackle it in this way, the Order belongs to you, and every stroke, being mentally handled, must become endowed with such poetry and artistry as God has given you. You alter one feature (which you have to, always), then every other feature has to sympathise and undergo some care and invention. Therefore it is no mean (game), nor is it a game you can play lightheartedly'*

*Edwin Lutyens (1903)*

Vibratory tone.

Disturbs the air, muffled jar dampened 'gainst insensate form.

Back and forth.

Swills consciousness inside throbbing head.

Harmonic oscillator, vibrates in single arc.

Rest.

Pause.

Repeat.

Wears thin the soporose veil that cowls the mind.

Breath.

Awaken.

Aaangg…

Retch of pumiced bile hangs acrid in the throat.

Rest.

Pause.

Twaanngg…

Stirring awareness of cold hard surface 'neath procumbent form. Unwilling eyelids creep ajar to let the light, double blink to blurred focus. Body rolls onto side loosing something from head. Push to sit dislodges to slipper-skim the face, tickle-twitch the nose, as falling free from pate tumbles black feathered crown.

Focus wander-roams from chaplet to distant near, lights upon black rust-tinged solleret, rests a beat…then resumes to rise up steel clad leg, pulling back to take in gaunt cloaked figure leaning lackadaisically against blackened stump. There cradled between knee and forearm, sweeping delicately above cascade of vertical strings, the twin slender curved recurve arms of a lyre.

From macilent knuckles the diligent extension of lithe gracilent finger to…

Definitely,

Meticulously,

Pluck a string.

Twaanngg…

**"Hello cherub."** Glints from pearly whites.

**"Timely as never it seems."** Half-stifled guffaw.

**"We knew you would get here in the end, but here is not there!"**

With dramatic sweep of cloak he gestures off into the distance, exposing a pauldron clad shoulder over which he slings the lyre. Then he is off like a shot striding clitter-clank into the vista.

Sight adjusts to take first real glance across strange terrain that I inhabit. Craggy islet of barren rock, forlorn landscape strewn with cold hard stones, boulders scoured by wind, abraded by time and dusted with delicate layer of pumiced ash, that softening contours like first flakes of drifted snow.

Yet the longer the eye alights upon one of these forms, the more it attunes to a geomorphic grace at odds with itself. For in their very unnatural natures are bred shades of the uncanny, of an unnatural beauty imparted upon the natural. Mind leads the eyes through slow dawned epiphany to paradigm shift of realisation, that this stark land no mere bleak outcrop, but ossuary for the unnatural natural, some macédoine charnel of masoned, carved, ornamental forms, laid to slumber under

limitless dark counterpane of welkin, shot through by patterned lume of distant stars.

Twaanngg…

His vibratory call to arms.

Twwwwaaaaannnnnnggg…

More impatient now.

Ahead of me on near rise of ground that forms the horizon he springs nonchalantly atop a pile of boulders, his silhouette cut Friedrichian 'gainst desolate sky. Sitting now, trying to gain the wherewithal to rise and follow my unlikely Virgil, I am struck with the odd sensation that I am about to fall. One cannot fall through solid ground, yet I have the feeling of being perched precariously at precipitous height, that one tiny move will have me teeter-totter and plummet. I stagger to knees mid reeling wave of nausea, stand through flowed ebb of tinnital shift and labyrinthital blow..

Twaanngg…

Strange comfort to be found in this tone that breaks the stillness of sound, that speaks to the senses but not to the eyes, that calming draws me to my feet to wend my path towards his form. Stepping up the rise I glance up at him.

"Most unusual feeling came across me, as if I were about to . fa…"

Tread from solid ground to nothing. Foot continues downward path, body diligently follows suit over precipital edge…

as I fall head first…

…then abruptly stop.

Senses shock-stung to activity leap to catch up with the swiftness of motion. Eyes scramble to focus as sight is swallowed by emptiness that stretches far beneath, more feeling than vision as all is swallowed by darkness of depth. This desolate promontory mere floating skerry above sideless abyss, some Prospero's isle above the void. The eye sweeps up expecting horizon that never comes, just more darkness, until straggled pin prick of stars betray some confused sense of up or down.

Never have I felt so small, so wretchedly alone, held there over such emptiness by some unknown force, nor known true depth till I stumble-fell from solid ground. Never had I known space till all was free from shape and form. And though my heart pounds within my chest there is no fear, but desire that wells from deep within, that curling tight twines round the bones and wrenches at my soul. This need that draws me out and down, that makes me crave the fall. L'appel du vide.

**"It's a long way down dearie!"**

Mellifluous tone, caramel for the ear.

Lifting me as if I weighed no more than a paper doll, he draws me up to the level of his eyes.

**"Shame to go before we've had a chance to chat, to catch up…hmm? It's been a while."**

Lowering my feet to terra firma he cedes his grip. Heart still beating fast, yet desire abates through touch of solid ground.

**"What is it they say? Look before you leap...Look before you leap... Ha ha! No matter!**

**"What a fine pair we make old chum, I some Simon Stylites pillared thus in ascetic wonder on this here vestigial berg, Chateau D'If to your sullen Dantès. We've seen some things you and I!"**

Sigh

**"What say you to a game?"**

"Ummm..."

**"Good, Gooood!"** He savours the words.

**"Let us take this rocky eminence, this lofty station for our Library of Alexandria. I some modern day Herodotus, you Callimachus of Cyrene. Let us make fresh our lists exalting the vaunted, those wonder of wonders...I'll start.**

**"First then to Ephesus and columned splendour. Ahh, sweet Artemisium, borne of Chersiphron and Metagenes, reduced to ash by Herostratic pride...**

**Now you."**

"Err...well...i'm not sure that I..."

**"Sharp as a tack as ever I see!...Fine, I'll go again.**

**"Next west to the peninsula, the Peloponnese. To Elis, to the temple, that we may once more anoint the ivoried skin there enthroned above dark reflective pool. Phidias' marvel, his god of gods, his Zeus..."**

Breath.

Words trail off, his face a sketch of tranquility, picture postcard of comfort yet loss. Though standing close he is so very far away, lost to currents of eddied reminiscence in former lives and distant times. One corner of his mouth rises to smile and somewhere deep within dark sunken eye sockets a spark struck catches kindling of idea, bursts to flame that building grows to raging fire, erupting from his mouth, spewn flow of molten words to break the silence.

**"But we more than mere scribes, you and I boy, for we may this very moment pull back the cloth that veils the past. Let us see for ourselves, be us Anubis or Aeacus, that we may in good faith judge and weigh their merits side by side.**

**"Sound the horn and beat the drum, awaken from slumber all those now gone, be they architect, sculptor, artisan, more. Let all come show us their plans, their works and their deeds. Let them raise up their ruins, bring them here to us now.**

**"Let us brush back the sands of time from rocky plateau of Giza, drawing forth from the earth the body of Hemiunu. Breathe back life to those arid bones that he may raise stone by stone from the necropolis, the Great Pyramid of Khufu in full glory here afore us.**

**"Come Pytheos, come Satyros, raise Mausolus' rest 'pon Halicarnassan heights. Let us place to one side the moon and the stars, let us shift each planet's orbit to give us some room, pluck the sun from its course and set as lanterned jewel to blaze afar 'pon Pharos' braziered spire.**

**"Phlegon, Aeos, Aethon, Pyrios, draw those burning rays across the sky, your chariot now mine cart to bear golden ores for the forges of Lindos. Let Chares fair hand cast bright garland wreath, radiate diadem to crown Helios, spoil of quake with broken knee, who rests beneath the waves. Come colossus rise once more to straddle harboured span.**

**"Let Nebuchadnezzar and Sennacherib, comets catch, and string to their bright tails fine spilling terraces to festoon the heavens with Babylon's lush swag!"**

My eye fixed on this most curious of orators, his body dervish now, wound wild in gesticulation crescendoed to match his words. Sweeping an arm in flourished gesture to take in vast sweep of empty sky, he leaps satyr-like from his rocky perch and comes to land with crashing metallic ring mere inches from my face. The hem of his cloak catches the soft layer of ash, whipping it up to envelop us like some poof of smoke from a stage prestidigitator.

'Ta da!?' I exclaim sotto voce to my self.

**'TAA DA! Indeed, my young stripling!'** Fortissimo misterioso reply through enshrouding haze hung lazy in the air, our nebulous illumined cocoon.

Breath.

Awareness of shadows that loom ahead through smokey hue.

Dust begins to settle, and there like prow of ship that cuts the wave a quoined cornice exposed to view through wisp filled air. Then as the mists break, filling the horizon as far as the eye could see are buildings. Architectural splendours from past millennia, crowded wall to gable, buttress to column, minaret to spire. Carved wonders from the past, within and without those venerated walls. Altars, statues, ornamental motifs, masterpieces of all styles and ages. Three hundred and sixty degrees crammed cheek to jowl, hanging, suspended silent in the air. No stone out of place in this panorama that surrounds our tiny isle, that overwhelms the eye and dizzies the mind.

With pealing carillon of laughter he joyfully slaps me hard on the back.

**'Well done lad, now this is more like it!'**

Hopping from one foot to another with childlike glee, he can barely contain his excitement. He begins to wander, pointing animatedly up and out at things that catch his eye.

**"Look in through the windows of the Hermitage, into the Louvre, but lo, empty of their spoils, for here the world as it was before it fell. See there Nike, winged Victory on her prow at Samothrace, and there Parthenons' fresh coloured pediment. No need for Elgin here, for our Mouseion is as far as the eye may see. Look, Pergamon altar, and over yon, lapis glow of Ishtar Gate. Study these sights with wandering gaze**

**that alights upon marvel. Stand there and narrate like Lemuel, of Brobdingnagian stature, taking all of Blefuscu and Lilliput in with one sweep of the eye. Describe for me what you see.**

**"Come, now let us make our lists!"**

With sinking creak to haunches a slender osteal finger becomes writing implement as he begins to scratch bold clear words into the dust.

*Temple of Bacchus.*

*Tomb of Theodoric.*

*Torre Asinelli.*

*Cathedrals- Freiburg, Mechelen, Frankfurt am Main.*

As the writing continues his eyes drift and rise from the ground, gaze focused intently on edifice laden sky.

*Choragic monument.*

*Erechtheum.*

*Karnak.*

*Lichfield Spire.*

Mumbling to himself he begins a rhythmic chant.

**"Architrave, anthemion, barmkin, bawn, bee-boll…"**

Breath

**"Boiseries, bucranium, cartouche, ciborium…"**

A draught of air begins to catch the contours of the scrawled letters,

**"Colonnade, colonette, columbarium…"**

blowing verticals to italic slant,

**"Corbie steps, cosmati work, crinkle-crankle wall…"**

perfect circles tilt ovoid,

**"Dalle-de verre, dosseret, en dèlit, grotto…"**

then loosing grasp of encircling form unclasp,

**"Feretory, flèche, gisant, herm, henge, hexastyle…"**

as letters fill and fall to obscure runes by his feet.

**"Lucarne, lunette, machicolations, metopes, narthex, nodding ogee…"**

pen-like finger moving now at frenetic pace,

**"Sheila-na-gig, souterrain, split-cusp, stylobate and squinch…"**

Echoed by the frenzied movements of his whole body that snakes this way and that.

**"Tempietto, terquetra, tas-de-charge, voussoirs…"**

To trample-tread over all that he has noted down.

Standing, unaware of his Sisyphean exploits, he turns to me voice tremulous with excitement.

**'Ah look betwixt the topless towers of Ileum, there the gloried work of Leochares, Bryaxis, Scopas of Paros, Timotheus… and there the temple of Asklepios!'**

With those words he stretches out an arm to lean his weight against the fragments of a precariously balanced fluted column.

**'You know old dear, I really feel that we cou…'**

The ancient section of column wobble-rocks upon its lower twin and with grinding sigh lamenting thus the final straw, cedes its long and delicate battle with gravity, and slides to topple the upper sections of column over precipitous edge to chasmic fall.

**'Ahh?!'**

As one we gawk anxiously over the edge to witness the sections of column tumble free from each other, down until they disappear enveloped by darkness.

Looking sheepishly at me he softly murmurs,

**'Perhaps maybe we can keep this one between you and I...eh?'**

I nod my assent.

Breath

A moment of change. Something has turned, now amiss, now askew. From distant temple movement. The corner column of grand portico buckles and in slow motion
drops from the sky…

its capital pitching free unseats entablature..

which cracking

splinter-breaks
the pediment

and falls away.
Gable front droop-sags in
upon
itself,
tegula strip
from imbrex,
flurried clay
confetti in the air,
as roof peels back to expose

pronaos,
cella,
adyton.

Ornament, statues,

all unhoused,

unmoored
from their
constancy.

Limbs

Snap-shatter
from
marbled bodies that shear diagonally
through catenary
folds of carved cloth,

stark decollations

as mosaiced floors ripple to tesseraed clouds

that burst

to
glinting torrents

and rain
down
into
the
darkness.

Like vast invisible wave that rending breaks over all that hangs afore us, wrought extirpation from some unseen hand. Sheltered in the the eye of this architectural hurricane, we bear witness as the firmament erupts. Manifest articulation of thought to form crumbles to decay as the world falls in slow motion.

**'Panta Rhei!'** he calls out.

**"And I Heraclitus, or fabled Nero as Rome burns below. Pass me my fiddle that I may strike a dirge... Too late! I've missed the dome of Hagia Sophia, there too crumples St Paul's, now Djoser's step pyramid, adieu Castillo de Kukulcan!...Quick boy, fetch me easel, hand me brush, take that stone by my foot as muller and crush that fine shingle 'neath us to pigment powder. Bring oils to mix kaleidoscopes of colour that I may stain canvas with this the final fall, for Martin did never paint such calamity or witness scenes stood so in cataclysmic awe!"**

Ere long it is over, all is lost, all is gone. Rent now of torrid motion, no trace left to mar the sky. Emptiness now hollow for we knew it not always so.

Sombre now the mood as he paces along the brink. There he comes upon a ring of stones, once plinths, long stood empty. Nine in all roughly hewn of no distinguishable time or style. Between them on the ground a long line of ornament fractured in the middle to dog-leg and divide the circle like the hands of a giant clock face.

**"Ah my favourite…egg and dart!"**

He falls into a slow step beside the line.

**"There was a time when such things would talk and whisper to us of universal truths. Each had a voice and could sing their songs that led back to a time when all was one.**

**"Egg, dart…**

**"Ancient times would reach forward from the past, extend their hands to us in their stories, their divinities, their gods.**

**"Egg, dart…**

**"And we reaching back would take those hands in ours, and touch those objects out of reach, those thoughts, those ages lost, through that mystical union of memory.**

**"Egg, dart…**

**"Yet in this endless cycle those days are lost and gone,**

**"Life, death…**

**"Till reaching into the abyss, nothing reaches back.**

**"Egg, dart…**

**"As time moves on and all is forgotten.**

**“Life, death…**

**“And we unmoored from the past should founder in the darkness, resigned to fall, to slake ones thirst and forget.**

**“Egg, dart…**

**“There are those who believe that this is the fate of the soul, their journey is one of forgetting it’s divine origins.**

**“Birth, rebirth…”**

Reaching the broken section he stops. There on dusty ground an egg sheared free from the surrounding moulding. Reaching to pick it up he eyes it intently.

**“Egg…**

**“Yet there are those few that stumbling in the tenebrous pitch should quenching drink from all that came before. Trembling though will steady themselves in their resolve, to raise a voice in the darkness and call upon the nine to raise their lamps with gentle glow, will slip their chains and light the path, and thus step forth to find another way.”**

Wandering back to bouldered rise I gaze out to caliginous swathe, and as my eyes fail to focus on the emptiness ahead of me he holds out the egg, dropping it gently to my cupped hands. Warm to the touch it brings comfort in the darkness.

Reaching within his cloak he pulls forth obsidian black the dusty spine.

Words falling fail from dusty lips, like hourglass trickled final sands, as fingers let slip his grasp.

**'The djed.'**

Peering over edge I watch till soon it disappears from view.

Stepping behind me, placing his hands upon my ribs to lift me beneath the arms, gently yet fully within his grasp. He hoists me up, pauses for one last brief tender moment, before casting me out into the darkness.

# Polyhymnia

interminably lost to ebb
and flow the glasslike veneer

away through an uncomfortable acquiescence

down upon
the velveteen
upon the ear. inner
comfort to be found
stillness of day to night,

speaks to the senses but not the eyes.
darkness reflected in the
water.

# Urania

Eye alights on some object half covered in dust, a small pebble worn smooth save several indentations on one side. Plucked swiftly up it is examined, turned once, twice within the hand.

**'Makapansgat..'**

Arm reaches back launching it to glistening arc across the sky. Through zenith peak to crescent dive slow begins to fall. Descends some time to graze the heavens, nine days and nights to pass the earth, nine more unto the pit. To rattling ricochet from guarded gates, through sealing grate of oubliette for those first damned. And clitter-clat upon the floor inciting stir from depths most Tartarine, the ichor of those derelict from humankind and time. They that dying not yet live no more, chained arm to arm to wait in darkened cell, turn gaze to this cobbled distraction. Now stand and raising arms through bronzed bars reach once more towards the sky.

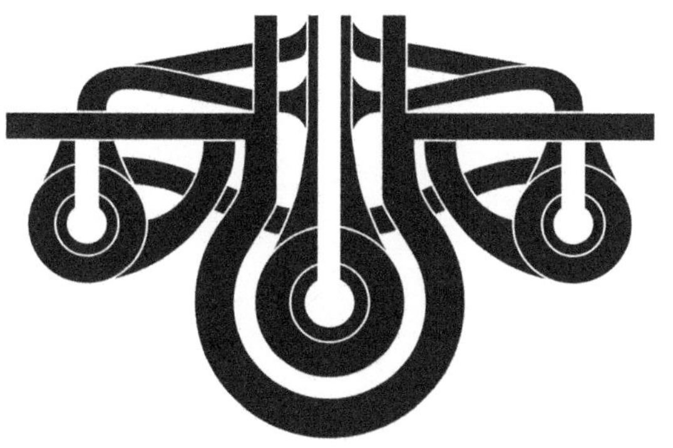

www.ingramcontent.com/pod-product-compliance
Lightning Source LLC
LaVergne TN
LVHW052354100826
845147LV00013B/839